Telling the Story

Telling the Story

Eight Christmas Monologues
and Poetry for Advent and Christmas

JODY SEYMOUR

RESOURCE *Publications* · Eugene, Oregon

TELLING THE STORY
Eight Christmas Monologues and Poetry for Advent and Christmas

Wipf & Stock
An Imprint of Wipf and Stock Publishers
199 W. 8th Ave., Suite 3
Eugene, OR 97401

www.wipfandstock.com

PAPERBACK ISBN: 978-1-5326-7355-9
HARDCOVER ISBN: 978-1-5326-7356-6
EBOOK ISBN: 978-1-5326-7357-3

Manufactured in the U.S.A.   FEBRUARY 27, 2019

This book is dedicated to the seven churches

I had the privilege of serving during my

forty-six years as a United Methodist pastor.

It was a joy to *tell the story*

to all of those dear people.

Contents

Acknowledgments | ix

Part 1 Christmas Monologues | 1

Introduction | 3

An Innkeeper Remembers | 5

Joseph | 10

A Shepherd Remembers | 17

A Wise Man Remembers | 23

Lost in Bethlehem | 30

Shaped by Love | 36

The Census Taker | 41

Herod | 47

Part 2 Advent Poetry | 53

Please Wait | 55

Not Yet | 57

An Advent Affirmation | 59

Beyond Impossible | 60

It Can't Be | 62

Still Christmas | 64

Too Full | 65

Part 3 Christmas Poetry | 69

Holding the Love of God | 71

In Spite Of | 74

Night Sounds | 76

Eyes Full of Light | 78

Joseph Make Me a Cradle | 79

Tired of Waiting | 81

The Wonder of It All | 83

She Wrapped Him Tight | 85

Wanting a White Christmas? | 86

No Room | 88

Manger Message | 89

Fear Not | 91

That Breath from Far Away | 93

The Cradle and the Cup | 95

Deep Was the Night | 97

Too Late | 99

Now It's Time for You to Sing | 101

God's Ponderings | 104

The Bethlehem Gazette | 106

Acknowledgments

I am grateful to Gail Spach, who lovingly
and conscientiously did the proofing
and editing of this book.

PART 1
Christmas Monologues

Introduction

AS A YOUNG PASTOR, I always fretted when it came time for Christmas. I felt a strange pressure to come up with something *really good*. I mean, Christmas is so special for so many people that what I offered needed to be *big*. After a while, it dawned on me that I could do no better than to tell the Christmas story itself. So, the next time that Christmas fell on a Sunday, I decided that I would simply *tell the story*.

My congregation at that time was mostly made up of young families with small children. The Sunday before Christmas, I told them that they could stay home on Christmas morning, enjoying opening presents and eating food. "However," I continued, lovingly chastising them, "if you do that, Santa wins and Jesus loses. Your actions will speak more than any words I could say, so I'll make you a deal: Get up early, open presents, and then come to church just as you are. The kids can wear their pajamas if they want to. Bring a present with you if you need to, and I promise you I will not preach. I will tell you a story."

Well, what a joy; they all showed up, many with pajamas on. I decided I would tell the Christmas story from the innkeeper's point of view. I donned a modest, biblical-looking outfit and became the innkeeper. It was magical. Everyone was with me.

But then I got to the part where the tired and frustrated innkeeper decided to open the door after a long interval of not responding to the constant knocks. Here's what the innkeeper said:

"I was tired of hearing all the excuses and lies: 'Please let me have a room; my child is sick.' 'Could you not find some space? It's cold outside.' 'I don't have enough money, but can you not find room in your heart for my family?' I don't know why I even went to the door. Maybe it was to let some cool air in because it had become musty with all the people in my too full inn. But I opened the door and there they were: a shabby-looking couple.

"The man was holding a rope tied to a donkey; the woman was bent over on the tired-looking beast. The man said, 'Please sir, could you find some room? My wife is about to have a baby.' My God, I thought, I have heard it all. Does this man think that I am supposed to believe that a man would take his wife out on a night like this if she is about to have a baby?"

As the innkeeper was saying all this, what he did not know was that four-year-old Teddy Gellar was standing on his tiptoes on the seat of the pew where he was supposed to be sitting. Teddy was really into the story, according to his mother who later recounted what happened. Just after the innkeeper shared his exasperation and disbelief, on hearing the words "Does this man expect me to believe such a story?" Teddy Gellar shouted out, "Yes!"

Well, you know how it is in church. Everyone was caught off guard, especially the innkeeper. There was a moment of silence, deep silence. The innkeeper froze, and then it happened. One person laughed, and then the whole crowd joined in loudly.

The innkeeper looked out at his audience with an expression somewhere between surprise and "what do I do now?" I smiled and laughed too. I guess I could have stopped right there and simply let people bask in the reality that Teddy had *preached the sermon by telling the story.*

Into all the "no" of that first Christmas night, Teddy had shouted out the punchline of the story. Are we to believe that the God of the universe chose to use a homeless couple to birth a love that came down from heaven? The answer is "yes."

Just so you know, the innkeeper regained his composure and continued on with the story. You can see how it all happened after Teddy's "Yes!" when you read the words of the first monologue in this book.

I offer you these first-person monologues as a way to tell the story. You will hear the Christmas story from eight perspectives: the innkeeper, Joseph, a shepherd, a Wise Man, a guest at a too full inn that night, a potter in Bethlehem, a census taker, and Herod. I also offer you some poems that I wrote in an effort to tell the story using the language of the soul: poetry.

T.S. Eliot once wrote, "We shall not cease from exploration and the end of all our exploring will be to arrive where we started and know the place for the first time" (*"Little Gidding," Four Quartets*). My hope is that as I tell the old, old story you will arrive again at the story and know it as if you were hearing it for the first time.

An Innkeeper Remembers

I STILL DO NOT know why I went to the door. I had long since ceased responding to the knocks that seemed constant. My wife had convinced me to allow more people to come in than our small inn could possibly hold.

Perhaps I went to the door to simply let some cool night in since the air inside was stale with the breath of the excuses I had heard the entire evening. "Please let me have a room; my son is sick." "I know you say you are full but there is nowhere else to go."

Then there were those who did not have enough to pay for a room but who convinced me that because of the heavy tax from the Romans we all shared the same plight. I was tired of the excuses and the lies.

I was prepared to respond to this knock late in the evening with pent-up rage, but when the light from the candle I was holding fell upon the faces of those at the door, my words of frustration froze in my throat. His eyes held desperation and her face was bent down. Her chin was almost buried in her chest, and I could see even as she slumped forward on the tired donkey that she was in some kind of pain.

I thought I had heard every excuse imaginable that night, but what he said next took the prize. "I know it's late but do you possibly have a room? My wife is about to have a baby."

What was in my mind was chastisement for this guy not having the foresight to see that such a journey was foolish. Sure, the registration was a necessity, but why bring your pregnant wife along? With the words still forming on my lips, I felt a tug on my sleeve.

"Abba, I put some fresh hay in the stall for Gamaliel. Can't they stay there? The woman seems to be so sad and hurt." Gamaliel was the prized lamb of my oldest daughter, Abigail.

As I looked back at Abigail, who should have been in bed, I heard the woman say, "My dear, you should be in bed. A little angel like you needs to be sleeping at such an hour."

I turned back toward the couple and told them they could indeed spend the night in our stable behind the inn. The man said "Thank you," and the woman reached down in her pain and patted Abigail on the head, "Go back to bed dear one."

Abigail, being the questioning child that she was, simply asked, "Why are you so sad?"

The woman attempted a smile and said, "Dear one, I am not sad. I'm going to have a baby tonight and I'm tired."

"Well, my name is Abigail. Abba says my name means 'source of joy.' What is your name?"

The woman leaned down toward Abigail and whispered, "My name is Mary. Now, you go to bed little angel."

Abigail turned and ran to where she slept. She literally had to leap over people who were sleeping in every space available in our inn. I felt almost embarrassed that I did not have a place for this dear couple because I had given in to so many others who had probably told me half-truths or lies.

I took them back to the stable and did what I could. I brought a bucket of water and some strips of cloth. As Abigail said, Gamaliel's stall was full of fresh hay. The playful lamb did not seem to mind being displaced for a time. There were more animals than usual in the stable since so many of the people filling my inn brought donkeys for carrying their goods and goats for milking.

"I'm sorry folks, but this is the best I can do at this time of night with my inn being so full because of the registration."

Mary looked up at me after her husband gently helped her off the donkey. "You are most kind. This must be God's will for us tonight."

I did not respond because lately I did not think much about God. Like most people in Bethlehem, I had grown tired of empty promises from ancient Scriptures that seemed to be void of meaning. I no longer observed the feast days and seldom went to the synagogue. What was true to me was the reality of constant Roman taxation. I no longer had any patience with the goings-on of rabbis who kept reading texts that told of a promised coming deliverer.

I wanted to say to this dear woman, "If you think it is God's will that your child be born in the midst of a bunch of animals, then you must have a different understanding of God than I do." I did not respond, however; I simply told them I hoped the night held something good for them.

When I returned, Abigail was standing in the doorway. In her hands was the blanket that her mother had woven for her earlier in the year. She always slept with that blanket. Abigail handed me the blanket, pulled me down toward her, and whispered, "Take this to Mary. She and her baby might get cold. Tell her . . ." and then she laughed softly, "Tell her an angel sent it."

I told her to get back to bed but I did not go back to the stable right away. It was later in the night, when I realized that sleep was not to be a part of this evening, that I ventured back to where they were.

As I approached, I could hear the sounds of a baby crying softly. I waited just beyond the light that came from the lantern I had given them. I turned and walked toward the light. Mary was leaning against the side of Gamaliel's stall. The man was hunched over a manger. He turned my way, and then I could see the child wrapped tightly in the bands of cloth.

"I see that the baby is here," I said, not knowing what else to say in what, at best, was an awkward moment.

"I'm Joseph," the man responded, "and your kindness this evening means so much to Mary and me."

Kindness? I thought to myself, you think my giving you a place in my stable for the birth of your child is kindness?

In a tired voice, Mary asked me, "Did Abigail ever go back to sleep?"

It was then that I remembered I was holding the blanket. "Yes, but before she went to sleep, she brought this for you . . . and for your baby."

I leaned down and gave her the message, "She told me to tell you it was a gift from an angel."

Mary smiled and reached toward the blanket. As she did this, she held my hand. Then she said, "Listen, I do not expect you to believe what I am going to tell you, but I feel I must at least say it."

As she folded the blanket and placed it over her knees, she looked into my eyes and said words I shall never forget, "Your little angel is not the only angel I have encountered of late." Then she closed her eyes and paused for a moment. Tears flowed slowly down her face.

In that waiting silence, I did not know what to say to this new mother who somehow thought birthing her baby in a stable was God's will and who seemed to be obsessed with talk of angels. Then she broke the silence, "I want you to look at him. The child in your manger is the long-awaited

Messiah. An angel promised me this. This stable this night holds God's child. I want you to know that. You have made a place not only for us tonight but for God."

I had no reason to believe such nonsense until I did what she asked of me. I turned and looked down into the manger. "Pick him up," she said. I'm not much for picking up babies. My wife always took care of this kind of thing, but somehow this seemed not to be not a choice but a necessity.

I picked him up and, well, I don't know what to say. A lot of things made no sense on this long night of mystery, so what I say now will also seem unreasonable. In his eyes was the light of stars. No, I do not mean the reflection of the bright stars that were shining that night. This was more than that.

In his eyes was something that reached up to me and held me. I have never had a feeling like that. My heart both pounded and ached. I had not had room for this? I had put God out back? I had met the long-awaited one with a greeting of "no"? Why did not some angel warn me? What does it mean that God would choose to come this way?

Mary was starting to close her eyes in much-needed sleep. As I put her child back down into the manger, she said to me as she pulled the blanket up over herself, "Tell your little angel I said thank you."

Behind me I heard something. I turned to see a group of shepherds kneeling just outside the stable. I heard one of them say to Joseph something about angels telling them to come. My God, this night was full of angel talk.

Just before I took my leave, I bent down to Mary and said, "Mary, is it really true? Can it really be?" She looked into my eyes and did not even need to respond. I knew. I knew.

I reached toward her and pushed some of the hay up around her weary body. As I pulled on the blanket to raise it higher up toward her shoulders, I said, "Mary, please keep the blanket as a gift for you and your child. After all, it is a gift from an angel."

Her lips parted in a slight smile and she spoke softly but one more sentence to me. I nodded my head in acceptance of her request.

As I walked back to the inn, the first glimpse of dawn was edging its way into the morning. In the doorway stood Abigail, waiting. "Abba, has Mary had her baby?"

I picked her up in my arms and held her close. My hand cradled her head against mine and I whispered, "Yes, Abigail, Mary had her baby. She asked me to tell my little angel that his name is Jesus."

Recommended music: "That Boy-Child of Mary."
Words and music by Tom Colvin.

Joseph

The Adopted Father

I wish you could have heard how he answered their questions! Twelve years old and he spoke as one who had mastered the many scrolls of our law. He spoke of the words of the prophets not like they were distant proclamations of former heroes; he recited their words as if they were something that he'd heard from his own family members at some gathering he had attended.

The looks on the faces of those learned men in the Temple were priceless. As I listened to him respond to them, I realized that some of the questions were asked in hope that one of them would finally make him stumble. Suddenly one of the scribes blurted out, "Who is this boy and where is his father?"

I proudly raised my hand and spoke, "I am his father. His name is Jesus, and we are from Nazareth."

"Nazareth?" responded the scribe, "How can this boy know so much if he was raised in Nazareth? I know the rabbi in Nazareth, and it's impossible that he could have taught your Jesus this much in such a short time."

"He's always been very bright." I smiled as I said those words.

Then I left him to continue his discussion. As I walked away to join Mary and the others, I could only imagine what these scholars of our Scriptures must be thinking as they listened to him speak of things beyond what any child could make up.

So it was that I was most embarrassed two days later when we were returning from Jerusalem to Nazareth after the festival. I assumed that Jesus was with some of my family. He was becoming hard to keep up with. He was beginning to spend more and more time away from us, and Mary and I knew that it was approaching the time that we would have to let him go his way.

When Mary asked me if I had seen him, I said no, but that I was sure he must be with Simon or Benjamin's family. Our search revealed no Jesus.

We turned and walked back to Jerusalem. We were worried, but I knew where to go. I found Jesus on the Temple steps again discussing some interpretation of one of the scrolls with those baffled priests and scribes. I listened for a moment as he expounded on some words from the scroll of Isaiah about the role of the suffering servant in God's plan to save the people.

It was then that I interrupted, "Son, you have caused much worry for your mother. Why did you not come when summoned?"

Jesus looked my way with eyes that seemed almost confused. His response did indeed bewilder those who had been listening intensely as this upstart boy interpreted ancient words. "Did you not know that I must be about my father's business?"

As he lowered his head and obediently walked over to me, one of the scribes said, "I thought you were his father?"

I started to respond to him but I knew there were no words that could contain any explanation. I simply looked down into my son's face as he smiled my way, reached for my arm, and said, "I am sorry father. I hope you understand."

Father: the sound of the word still echoes in my memory. These carpenter hands have crafted so many things, but the finest thing in my life I did not make. I am an adopted father.

I loved her from the moment I first saw her drawing water from the well at the edge of Nazareth. I did not want to grow old alone; I wanted so much to be a father. The people of Nazareth all treated me with respect, but none of them knew the deep longings that dwelt within my heart.

After all, I was Joseph the carpenter who fashioned their tables and chairs and the cradles for their children. I was the elder who was often asked to read the Scriptures in our synagogue. My not being married was to them a sign of my independence and strength. Perhaps I had given myself to my work and my role as leader of our village so much that, as folks sometimes said, "Joseph does not need the love of a woman nor does he need children to sleep in his cradle."

They were wrong. It surprised some when I signed the contract of betrothal along with Mary's father. I paid him the customary amount to acquire her. Mary was present for the blessing of the contract. The rabbi said the ancient words and Mary looked up at me only once. It was a look of respect. How I wanted so much more from her deep eyes, but what could I expect? She was the property of her father, and she was simply there to complete an arrangement. She would remain in her father's house until the day of our wedding.

Mary and I would take walks near her home. I told her that our wedding would be a gala event, and I promised to provide a good life for her, or at least as good as one could expect in our poor village. Mary would only nod and try to smile. She said very little to me, and since I was so much older, she treated me more as a father than as one who would be her husband.

How I wished there was more in her heart for me. I had made an arrangement but what I desired was a relationship. Mary knew that she was betrothed to a man who was respected and who was a leader, but I wanted something more than just respect for a man who was seen as righteous and upright. No one knew these feelings of mine but God and me.

Ah, God, this is where things got complicated. I will never forget the day Mary came to me in the early morning. It was not acceptable within our custom for her to come to my house unaccompanied, so I was surprised to see her. She stood in my doorway as the new day's sunlight came over her shoulders. The morning light behind her made her look radiant, but then she always looked radiant to me.

As she stepped my way, I could tell that she had been crying. I wanted to comfort her, but we were still only acquaintances and the marriage was months off. I lived in the hope that she would learn to at least want to love me. Her next words almost stopped my longing heart:

"Joseph, I do not know what words to use to tell you this: I am with child."

Hearts break in many ways. Mine was already wounded from too many years of being alone. Now my Mary had ended all hopes for a future, a future with someone who would fill my solitude, even if it was just an arrangement.

After the pain came the fear, fear for her. I knew what the scrolls of our law said. Such an act of adultery by a virgin who was betrothed was an abomination. According to the scroll of Deuteronomy, I was to report the act to her father who then could take her to the gates of our Nazareth and have her stoned to death by the village elders for the sin. My Mary, an abomination! I wondered if Mary even knew the words of our ancient law. She was so young, and of course, being a woman, was not allowed to hear the words of the law that were read by people like me in the synagogue.

I knew my other choice was to negotiate with her father. I could ask him to keep the money that I had paid for Mary's betrothal and convince him to use part of it to arrange a private divorce. I could then ask him to take Mary from Nazareth for a while so she could have the child away from the stares and the whispers that would surely come.

I was lost in this dialogue within my mind when Mary reached her hand out to me and held my hand so softly. How I had longed for her to do that, but now it would not matter. Then she spoke words that were beyond imagining: "O Joseph, it is not what you think. One evening, weeks ago, the light of our God overwhelmed me, and a voice said to me that I would be the mother of the Messiah. I told this messenger that I had not yet been with you, but the voice said to me that God's spirit would do this. I do not know why God chose me, Joseph. I am both filled with fear and joy at the same time. I am sorry, Joseph, for I cannot expect you to understand."

She turned and walked away into the morning. I wanted to be angry. I wanted to scream at how cruel all of this was. Had I not tried to be faithful and patient? What kind of message must this be from God? I could not imagine my Mary being with someone else, but then I knew the impossibility of what she was saying. Somehow anger could not find a place in me. I believe it was because there was so much love for Mary within me that there simply was no room for anger.

The next few nights were sleepless. All I could think of were the words I would need to put together to explain to Mary's father what needed to be done so that Mary could escape as much pain as was possible. I knew that because of my role in our village I could convince her father that my decision to privately divorce her would be best for the family. I would not allow him to act on his sense of betrayal by his daughter. Stones of judgment would have to remain on the ground.

One night, however, I somehow managed to sleep. It was a restless sleep. I smile now as I think of that night and I remember how our ancestor Jacob wrestled with his angel. After that encounter by the river Jabok, Jacob's life and name were changed. After my encounter this night, my life was forever changed.

The voice in the night came to me like water that broke through a dam. At first it was almost like the piercing words from Mary's announcement telling me that she was going to have a child that was not mine. The words this time though were haunting, "Do not be afraid to take Mary as your wife, Joseph. The child is mine."

"The child is mine?" "What does that mean?" I said to the darkness. "Whose child is this? *Mine*? Who is *mine*?" I wanted *mine* to be mine.

I realized, even in my dream-like state, that my words made no sense. None of this made any sense. Then there came the silence, the deep silence. The silence was penetrating like the look in Mary's eyes. The silence spoke words. It was then that I realized whose Mary's child was. Do not ask me to explain this. I then knew what I was to do.

How this could be no longer mattered. I simply knew it was true.

This time I surprised Mary and her parents with my visit. I was allowed by custom to request to be alone with Mary. Her father quickly granted my request. I could tell by his manner that he did not yet know of Mary's news. Mary walked beside me but she would not look at me. We walked in silence for a while. I took her to the well where I first saw her. No one else was there.

"Mary, I don't think you are aware of the very first time I saw you draw water from this well. As I looked at you, I hoped we could one day be married. For months I waited and then arranged with your father for us to be betrothed. You are mine, Mary."

She looked down into the darkness of the well. I reached toward her chin and gently lifted her eyes towards my own.

"I am not talking property rights, Mary. I do not care about the legal arrangement or the customs. You are mine, Mary, because of my love for you. You are mine because I need your love."

She looked at me questioningly, so I continued, "I found my angel last night, Mary, or did my angel find me? I know I am not the father, Mary, but I know who the father is. Mary, can I be our son's adopted father?"

Then her eyes looked not at me but into me. Her tears came first. She did then what I had only dreamed of her doing. She leaned into my chest and slowly put her arms around my shoulders. She said nothing for a few long moments. I could only feel her gentle sobs.

Then she leaned back and looked at me. She cupped my face in her soft hands and said, "O my Joseph, how I will need you. Our son needs a father."

Words cannot hold meaning sometimes. Her words were so full that the meaning broke open. No vessel could contain what she tried to say. Her words "O my Joseph" were words that filled my ache and my longing, and those words "our son needs a father" completed my life.

I took Mary to my home as was allowed by our custom. Her pregnancy then became acceptable, and the whispers could be put in their place.

In the evenings after I finished my work, I would put my head on Mary's swelling abdomen. I watched the movement of what must be a knee or an arm. I smiled as she winced at such play within her.

When I told her of the news that I would have to return to Bethlehem because the hated Romans had again declared that we must register for more taxes or face the consequences, Mary announced that she was going with me. I told her that there was no way she could manage such a three-day journey in her condition.

In a family, the husband's word should be the final word, but you do not know my Mary. She looked at me and said that she could not be without me no matter what. She said this must somehow be part of God's plan. I can deal with God on one hand and Mary on the other hand, but I cannot manage both God and Mary.

That was it and I knew it. It took us five days to make the journey to Bethlehem because we had to stop so much. Her pain was becoming something that had to be listened to.

We arrived late in the evening. By this time, Mary was holding onto our tired donkey's neck and leaning into her pain. As I negotiated with the innkeeper who kept telling me that sleeping space was long since occupied, I pointed to Mary's condition.

He shook his head in wonder and motioned for me to follow him. "Look, my wife died a few years ago. I have no one to send back here to help you and your wife through this. I will bring you water and some cloth. That is the best that I can do. This is indeed a godforsaken time."

I thanked him. Mary looked up at me through her pain and then around at the animals in the stable. She managed a smile and only said, "God is full of surprises, is he not, my Joseph?"

"Yes, Mary," I said, "I suppose you and I should be used to being surprised by now."

The innkeeper brought me the promised water, some strips of cloth, and a lantern. As he turned to walk away, I simply said to him, "After tonight this time will not be so Godforsaken." He looked back at me and nodded. I knew he did not understand my words, but then who would be able to understand any of this?

Mary's labor was not long but it was hard. I did not know what to do but I did it. Men were not supposed to do such things. It was ritually unclean for me to help with childbirth, but then this was not an ordinary evening. If I could not be there in the making of our child, I was to be there at his birth.

He was born early in the morning before the sun came up. I wrapped him in the bands of cloth I had cut and handed him to Mary. Her swollen face smiled at me and at him as she nursed him. There can be no more precious sight than a mother nursing a child, especially this child. She then gently rocked him in her arms. His eyes closed.

The night was still and the animals seemed to act as a quiet witness to the moment that was to change everything. Then Mary looked up at me, "Joseph, here is your son." She handed him to me and we shared a knowledge that no one else could share.

His eyes opened ever so slightly and he looked at me. "I take you as my son, O little one, though you are not of my making."

As I laid him in the manger close by, I looked at Mary who was trying to rest in the place where one of the cows had been sleeping.

I gazed down into the manger and said to our son, "Your name shall be Jesus. A father always names his child so here, today, I give you this name, Jesus." And then I glanced toward Mary and back to Jesus and said, "O child of mystery, your father gave me your name one evening in my dreams, and though that father shall always be yours, so shall I be your father also."

I heard a noise behind me and noticed a group of shepherds walking toward us. I wondered what they must want. Mary, turning to me, said, "O my dear Joseph, thank you for listening to your dreams. I need you to be a father to our Jesus for I sense in my heart that his other father has much for our child to do, some of which already causes fear to well up in me. For now, hold him in your hands, those wonderful hands that have crafted so much for others. Hold him in your hands, my dear Joseph, for he is your child too."

Recommended music: "Joseph's Lullaby."
Words and music by Fred Pratt Green and Russell Schulz-Widmar.

A Shepherd Remembers

MY FATHER GAVE IT to me when I was twelve years old. That's how old a shepherd is when he receives his own staff for the first time. It means you are old enough to be in charge of the late-night watch by yourself. Each one of our staffs is different, and they represent who we are. Usually it is our fathers who choose the particular branch of the tree from which the staff will be carved. A shepherd's staff is really special, and we use the same one all our lives.

But for a long time, I did not have my own special staff. You see, I gave it away, and only much later did I get it back again. Many years have gone by now, and that once-eager-twelve-year-old body is worn out from long nights of standing watch on the hillsides. But I'm not too weary to share with you the story that changed my life so long ago.

That night, it was my turn to keep watch while the others were sleeping. The air was clear and a bit cold. Leaning on my new staff, I knew that I must be careful not to fall asleep. We shepherds love our sheep, but we also know how careless they can be. One of them will often wonder off in search of most anything, a distant patch of grass, a sound that leads their curiosity to places where they can fall into deep crevices, and then one of us has to go to get them out. They sometimes just don't pay attention.

And then there are the wolves that prey on the flock. Over my years, I have had to fend off fierce attacks that would have wreaked havoc on the sheep. For many of those years, the staff I used to defend our sheep was not this one, but I'm going to tell you about that in a while.

To this day, I cannot really explain what happened late that night as I stood alone watching our sheep. All of a sudden, I started hearing voices, and they seemed to be coming from, well, the sky. It was one of the brightest evenings I could remember.

At first, I thought it was the wind making its way through the small trees and undergrowth. I thought perhaps I had drifted off to sleep only to awake in the midst of some dream. But then the voices grew louder, and all I can say is that it was as if the stars started coming closer and becoming brighter.

I was new at this being alone with the sheep and being responsible for their safety. I had to keep my senses. At first, I wanted to run back to the others, who were asleep around the embers of the fire, but I knew they would consider me filled with childish imagination.

But my choice was made for me when the light became so bright that it woke my father and the other shepherds. Of course, it was not just the light; it was the voices, the singing, and the words.

I looked around, behind me, and there stood the others. No one said anything; there was nothing to say. As we listened, fear became our companion. The light became almost blinding.

And then came words, "To you is born a Savior . . . Do not fear . . . Go down to the town below and find him . . . He is the one you've been waiting for . . . And so that you will believe, here is a sign for you . . . The child will be in a manger . . . Go . . . Tell everyone you meet what you have seen down in the city of David."

Then the voices filled everything. They filled us. There are no words to describe what we heard. The only thing I can remember, because we kept hearing it over and over, was "Glory to God, Glory to God!"

We all knew that the instructions made no sense. We were not welcome in any town. Below us was Bethlehem, but we knew that to go there was to risk ridicule. The religious leaders considered us unclean, and most people assumed we were thieves and vagabonds. We were accustomed to such accusations

My father had helped me understand that to be a shepherd was to have no place that was really home, except to be with each other and our sheep. The people in those towns had no use for us, despised us even, but what they did need from us was our sheep. They paid us for them for their religious sacrifices. If anyone asked where the sheep had come from though, we were to be invisible servants. Those who bought our sheep had no understanding that we loved the sheep as a parent loves a child but that it was our way of making a living.

So why did those voices from heaven come to us? No one would believe the story about what we had heard and seen, especially coming from the lips of shepherds.

Although my father was not allowed to go to the synagogue, his own father had taught him the stories of our faith. My grandfather had been befriended by a rabbi. This religious scholar was a kind man, and though my grandfather could not read the words on the sacred scrolls, the rabbi had read them to him and for him.

So, my father said to me, after the voices seemed somehow to go back into the heavens from where they came, "Son, these voices tell of the one I told you of. Your grandfather told me what the rabbi taught him. This child is the one we have been waiting for. This manger child is the deliverer."

I looked into his eyes and said words I now hold near to my heart, "But father, how is it that we are the ones invited? The child is surely not for us."

My father's words still live with me in spite of the years gone by. He said, "O my son, that is what is so wonderful. It seems that we are the first to know. The rabbi told my grandfather and my father told me that the Promised One would be a shepherd for his people and that he would especially come for those who were forsaken and on the outside. Do you now see why shepherds are the first to know?"

We went to the town as the voices instructed. I was afraid we might be driven away as we had been before in other towns, but it seemed that all of Bethlehem was asleep. My brothers told me of the census and how so many had come into this tiny village, so I was surprised that the town was so quiet.

"How will we know where to go?" I asked my father.

"I'm still hearing the voices," is all he said. We led our sheep to the edge of the town, and it was there that my father pointed with his staff to a lantern burning in a stable. I remembered that earlier the voices said the child would be found in a manger, so we walked toward the light.

She was bending over the manger when I first saw her. She looked up and did not even seem surprised to see us. A man was standing behind her. My father stepped forward and spoke some words to him. It was then I saw the man smile and gently shake his head.

I leaned against my father's strong back and stood on my tiptoes to see what I could see. There he was, the manger child. Something came over me like the fires that sometimes break out in the valleys when the grass is dry.

As the others in our band knelt down near the manger, I stepped forward. My father motioned for me to step back, but I was lost in the wonder of it all.

I walked over to the woman and said simply, "My father said that your child would grow up to be a shepherd, a very special shepherd. He will need a staff. This staff is very special to me. It's mine, but I want your shepherd to have it. When he gets older, tell him that another shepherd gave it to him on the night of his birth."

She looked into my eyes with something that I can only describe as love in motion. She reached toward me and gently put her hand to my cheek. She spoke in a tired whisper, "I know this staff must be valuable to you, so what a gift it is. I will keep it and give it to him when it is time for him to tend his sheep."

As time went by, I grew up and became the lead shepherd of our gathered families. It was my task to sleep sometimes in the opening of the stone enclosure we call a sheepfold. That way I was the gate through which the sheep must pass. I kept the sheep in and the wolves out. Any person or predator would have to get past me to get to the sheep.

Consequently, the words he spoke that day so many years later sank deep into my soul as I heard him talk about being the good shepherd who was the gate for the sheep. I had tried to keep up with his whereabouts and his teachings. Word had spread quickly about the way he could touch people and heal them.

Rumors of him quieting storms and even changing water into wine were spreading among the many people who came to hear him speak in order to discover if he really was the long-awaited one. Very few of those people knew of the night of his birth even though we told everyone who would listen. Most people did not believe us, so it was only much later after he chose followers and started teaching that people began to ask if he really was the deliverer.

I would go listen to him whenever I could get away from the sheep. The crowds were often so large that I had to struggle to get close enough to hear his words. And if the religious leaders were present, I had to worry about their judgmental stares, but I decided that did not matter anymore. I was tired of being viewed as one who was not worthy. After all, I knew who he was before they did, even if they did not believe our stories of stars that sang and voices in the night.

So it was that one day, as I was listening to him, he told the crowd gathered around him that he was the good shepherd and that he had come to be the gate through which the sheep could come home. As he said those words about being a shepherd, my heart sang like that night long ago, when it seemed that angels had broken loose from heaven. His closing words were the ones I remember most. He had stopped speaking and became silent for what seemed like a long time. He looked off into the distance as if his mind was far from the place.

Then he looked back at the people, who had been listening to him intently, and said, "The good shepherd lays down his life for his sheep." It was at that moment that I noticed the staff in his hand. My old eyes filled with tears. It was my staff. I looked down at my feet and prayed softly, "O God, may my staff help him lead us."

When I looked up, he was standing in front of me. I could not believe that this was the child of the manger, the one whose mother I had offered my shepherd staff to so long ago.

He put his hand on my shoulder and smiled. "You're the one, aren't you?" Before I could answer, he said, "My mother told me of that night and of how you were the first to come. It was one of her favorite stories to tell because of what you gave to her. I have used this staff these years not only to lean on but to, well, to try to be a good shepherd."

That's when we both smiled a smile of recognition that only the two of us could share, shepherd to shepherd. Then he did something that allows me to tell you this story. He handed me back my staff and said, "I want you to have this now. I'm going to Jerusalem and will not be coming back this way so I want it to be yours again."

I wanted to argue with him and tell him that the gift was his to keep, but somehow the words did not come. As he turned to walk away, he smiled and said to me, "You are a good shepherd too, you know."

Word came to me later about what they did to him in Jerusalem. What did he do to deserve crucifixion? I will never understand why they killed a man who came to be the long-awaited shepherd for us all. Did they not know how much we need a shepherd?

Some people claim that death could not hold him and that when grieving followers returned to his grave, they found the tomb empty. Others say it is just wishful thinking by people who hoped he was what he was not.

But I know who he was and who he is. I was one of those lucky shepherds on a hillside who were told to go down to a town to discover a shepherd born in a manger. As I hold my staff, his staff, I thank God that I was able to stand that night long ago beside a manger on ground that was holy. Voices that seemed like those of angels told us surprised shepherds to go tell the story about what we would see. So, hear these words of a tired old shepherd who once gave his staff to the shepherd who came to save us all. He is the manger child who is the good shepherd.

I'm one lucky shepherd . . .

Recommended music: "More Than a Child."
Words and music by Lawrence Keith Holder.

A Wise Man Remembers

THE LONGING WAS ALWAYS there. As a child, I remember looking to the stars and wanting to find something that seemed always to be missing. I would stand close to the map room where the sacred scrolls were kept. I was not allowed in because I was constantly reminded that, even though I possessed an obsessive curiosity, I was still nothing but a child and needed to remember my place.

My father was the leader of our tribe, and everyone knew that one day I was to take his place. Our tribe was greatly respected for our collection of sacred scrolls from all over the world. We were known not only for our knowledge but for our ability to interpret dreams. Generations of our people studied the sacred texts from many nations, and over the years we collected and studied maps that told of ways to go to far countries.

Our understanding of stars and their meanings were what made us most respected. Kings would send emissaries to seek our interpretations of star movements to see what they might tell of coming events. I would hide behind the columns that were next to the door of the sacred room. I longed to know what the stars were saying to me.

One evening, one of the elders caught me listening to their conversation. As he chastised me for being where I should not be, I noticed that my father placed his hand upon the shoulder of his companion. My father simply said, "Let him be."

"But he is nothing but a child and should not be in this place."

"But he is *my* child and one day he will be standing where I stand. His eagerness may be inappropriate to you, but it may just be part of what kind of leader he will be some day." Then my father bent down and looked into my eyes. He said nothing, but he invited me into that room with the maps and the charts.

One side of the massive room had an opening in the roof where the stars could be viewed and studied. I will never forget that very first night that I was invited into that place even though I was, to the elders, nothing but a child. I recounted this story years later as I paid tribute to my father beside his grave.

Now I am the one that people look to for pathways to the future. So, it was a surprise when I called into that sacred space some of my fellow seekers after truth to discuss with them what I had discovered.

I rolled out some of the scrolls I had been studying and told them I was preparing to take a long journey. They were immediately troubled. They quickly informed me that there were others I could send to discover what I was seeking. My place was as the leader of my people. Journeys to other lands could be dangerous. There were bandits and the ever-present challenge of finding food and water in some places.

"I go to find a new king," I said.

"You do not need to find a new king," one of my companions responded, "You must stay here and be our king and leader."

"No, I must go. I somehow feel that this journey is part of the longing that I have possessed since my childhood."

"How do you know this is what you should do?"

It was then that I led them to the place where the night sky could be seen. I simply pointed upward. They were silent.

"When did this appear?" one of them said. "How can a new star simply come from nowhere?"

I answered simply, "It is a star that I know I must follow. You might say it is *my* star." Then I rolled open the scroll and told them that actually it was *his* star.

"What do you mean?"

I read them the ancient words from the scrolls we had collected from the people called "Hebrew." "A star shall come out of Jacob, and a scepter shall rise out of Israel."

"What does that matter to us?"

"It matters to me," I said. "I have been dreaming about this star and this king. I have searched these people's scrolls and find a mystery indeed. The new king will also be a shepherd. There are words that tell that he may even be wounded for his people's transgressions."

"What kind of king is that?"

"That is what I must know," I said.

"These people whose words promise a king. Do they really want a king?"

"That is one of the problems. You see, they do have a king, but he is a ruthless bloodthirsty imposter of a king who has killed his own children and one of his wives. King Herod uses their religion as a shield, but he understands it not, I think. But we must first go to him before we find this other king."

"Now you are speaking in riddles rather than with the wisdom we know you for."

I think my traveling companions came with me more to make sure I returned safely rather than to discover what I was searching for. My dreams kept surrounding me with hope that I would discover something or someone that would match the depth of my strange longing.

I studied both ancient texts and our star maps and I prepared gifts fit for a king. Logic would have it that the one known as the "King of the Jews" would be found in their sacred city of Jerusalem, a name that means *City of Peace* but a city that in fact knew so much strife.

One of the reasons I wanted to find this new king is that one of the prophecies I had discovered said that the new king would be a prince of peace and a wise counselor. These strange people who I discovered worshiped only one God sure needed such a king. After studying their history, I discovered that they were a people who wandered away from truth so often that I wondered why any God would care to save them, as was predicted that this new king would do.

And then there was Herod who wore the crown, though he had purchased it with money and blood. We went first to him for I knew our search would eventually come to his attention. His reaction was a strange one. He was fascinated at our knowledge and our grasp of the language of his people. We knew many languages and studied many of the ways, customs, and religions of those who wanted to discover truth.

He told us he too wanted to know truth and that if indeed our research indicated that a king would be born, he needed to be able to kneel at the feet of that king. His scholars and priests had told him that such an event had been prophesied, although his people had long given up on these ancient words of hope.

He then looked out an open window and gestured toward the city below. He said that in order to rule he would need to pay homage to this new king because their religion spoke of this king being sent from the one true

God. Herod knew how to use words to make people think he truly cared for his people, but what he did not know is that I knew his history.

Herod wanted to know exactly when we had discovered the star and what we thought it meant. He then informed us of what his priests and scholars had discovered and that the king was probably already born, but not where we imagined.

One of his priests pointed to a scroll and started to read the words, but I saw where he pointed and surprised him when I read the words: "And you, Bethlehem, in the land of Judah, are by no means least among the rulers of Judah, for from you shall come a ruler who is to shepherd my people Israel."

In the silence that followed I pondered what this meant. Bethlehem was known as the city of David. David was the greatest king that this strange nation had ever had. My studies revealed that as a child the young David had been a shepherd. It was later that he became a mighty warrior who united his people for the first time into what would become a nation to be reckoned with. But then the people had become unruly yet again and were defeated and led into exile. Jerusalem was destroyed and the Temple left in ruins.

David became a symbol of the days of glory, and people longed for another David. What they got, however, was Herod, who prided himself in rebuilding the Temple. The Temple was an amazing structure, and its beauty was known throughout the region, but its mighty towers and inner-most sacred place, called the Holy of Holies, could not cover up the deceit of the king who built its walls.

I knew that Herod's desire to find this new king was so that he could do what he had done with anyone who threatened his reign. His words of welcome to us included his request that when we found the new king, we should return to him so that he could do him honor.

I assured him we would do so, knowing that I would never play into his scheme to maintain a rule that surely needed to be ended. We were but actors on Herod's stage to carry out a plot that would again make it look like Herod was abiding by a religion that he used only for his own gain.

I played his game and acted a part but knew in my heart that what I longed for was far from what Herod wanted or needed. I told him that we would continue our search the next night, but when we left his chambers, I informed my companions that we would leave Jerusalem immediately and secretly if possible.

I knew that Herod's only intention in seeking this new king would be to destroy him. There was one too many stars in Herod's sky, and there was no room for another king.

We arrived at Bethlehem early in the evening. We were conspicuous because of our dress and our camels bearing supplies. I walked up to a person sitting on a large stone outside one of the small huts in the village. People seemed to be leaving the small village.

I asked, "Where are the people going?"

"They are going back home after registering for yet another tax."

"Who in your village would be able to tell me the most about what is really happening?" I asked.

"What do you want to know?"

"We are seeking the one who is born king of the Jews."

"King of the Jews? You need to go to Jerusalem, good sir. We already have a king, such as he is."

"Please, I ask your patience. Is there someone in the village who would know what has happened, say in the past few days?"

"Go see Benjamin, the old man over there beside the inn. He has lived here all his life, and I heard him telling some wild tale the other day about shepherds who saw angels and heard voices. Nobody believes him, but you seem to want to hear about strange things."

I approached Benjamin. He was carving what looked like a small image out of a piece of olive wood. He looked up at me. "Have you come to find a king?" My other two traveling companions could not believe his words; I could tell from their expressions.

"Well, yes we have," I said.

"I kind of thought some folks like you might show up. I feed the animals each night at the stable behind this inn, been doing the same all my life. The other night in the midst of the madness of this foolish registration, I found this man and a woman in the stable. She was leaning over something and the man was holding a lantern. I started to shout at them about why they were in there, when I saw the baby in the manger.

"Before I could say something, some shepherds came up behind me and knelt in front of the manger. I wondered what in the world was going on there. Then, one of them started talking about angels and the Messiah being born and that they were to come and find him in a manger. You know, people here think I don't know much, but I know what my father kept telling me about the coming one.

"I walked over to the manger next to the kneeling shepherds, looked down into the hay and, well, don't know how to say this to you, but I knew he was the one. I remember my daddy telling me that one day a new king would come, just didn't figure he would come in a stable. When I looked over at you three talking to Michael, I said to myself, Bet they've come from someplace far off to find a king.

"But he is not in the stable over there anymore. Some folks found out about them and offered them a place in that house just over there. I guess they figured a stable was no place for a king."

We walked over to the house. I took from the skins that were hanging on the camels the gifts I had brought. I handed one gift to each of my companions, who by this time could say nothing.

I knocked on the door. A woman came to the door and stepped back almost in fear. I looked over her shoulder and saw a younger woman holding a blanket near to her breast.

I did not wait for an invitation to enter the house. My two companions followed me. The mother of the child looked up into my eyes. There was no surprise or shock in her eyes to see us standing there.

She simply looked up at me from her small stool where, I assume, she had been nursing the child, and said, "You have come to see him, haven't you? How kind of you. I see from your robes and fine garments that you must be very special people."

"We are Magi from the East, O fair one. We have come to pay homage to a new king for we have seen his star over our skies, and we come now to give you gifts in his honor. Here is gold for his rule; here is frankincense to honor him as a priest to his people; and here is myrrh for you to save for his royal funeral someday. I understand from reading your sacred texts that he is to be a king and yet a shepherd to his people."

We knelt in front of her.

"O great ones who are wise enough to follow stars, all I can tell you is that an angel first told me of this child, and shepherds knelt in front of a manger where I laid him for his first night in our world because they said angels told them to, and now you come because of a star that brings you from your home. Yes, he is the one you seek, and though I know you have come far and what you now see is nothing but a child, he is the king, the shepherd. You were right to follow his star."

As we turned to leave, one of my companions whispered to me, "Did you know that we would travel all this way and find *nothing but a child*?"

Hearing these words, I remembered what the doubters had said when, as a boy, I hid outside my father's map room door longing to overhear the wisdom of those who studied the stars. I was full of curiosity and eager to learn, but they had found me wanting to know so much before they had deemed it time and said these same words, "He is nothing but a child."

In that moment, as I looked back toward his mother, I knew that for a time I was a child again. And it was then that the deep longing that had lived within me since my youth was met by a feeling I had never had.

It was as if a dream had been realized. My search was over and it was made complete by one who was what I once was, *nothing but a child*, but he was *the* child.

Recommended music: "Nothing but a Child" by Steve Earle.
Sung by Kathy Mattea.

Lost in Bethlehem

A Weary Visitor at the Inn

THE LIGHT LEFT ME two years ago. The Scriptures taught to me as a child by the rabbi in my village spoke of a day when the stars would fall from the sky. He called it the "Day of the Lord," and he warned the small group of boys who gathered at his feet to learn Torah that God would judge his people if we did not learn his ways and keep his commands.

I wondered even then if God had not already judged us or even left us to our own devices as I looked all around to see Roman soldiers patrolling our neighborhood and taking our money with their dreaded taxes. Why wait for the light to fall from the sky when it seemed that Caesar and his cronies like Herod had robbed us of both the warmth and the light?

But all that changed years later when I met Rachael and she gave me our child, Aaron. He became the light of my life. I remember the day of his dedication when the rabbi lifted him up to God and spoke his name for the first time to the people gathered. That day "alleluias" rang out in the small room that was our synagogue. Never had the meaning of the word become so clear to me. In our language, "alleluia" means "offer praise to God."

Aaron was my way to put the stars back in the dark sky of what life had become under an enemy occupation. But then came the time that the stars fell from my sky and the alleluias I longed to offer God became silent. The fever that came to our village took many. We were helpless in the face of whatever unnamed disease this evil visited upon us.

With no money to buy the strange herbs and spices that some used in the face of such fevers we simply watched as the light left us. I held Aaron and bathed him with cool water. Rachael was weak from battling the demon herself. She whispered to me many times that all would be well. Her faith often exceeded mine. She knew from the beginning that my faith was a struggling one. I had a hard time believing what I had been taught as a child by my religious teachers.

They had spoken of promises that one day the light would shine in the darkness and that God would deliver us. As I held Rachael's burning hand, she would still smile and say, "All will be well." All I could do was look back at her with love laced with fear and say nothing.

Aaron died in my arms. I am not sure if Rachael died from the burning in her bones or the grief in her heart, but I lost her a few days later. All was darkness and silence.

I asked God to take me and shook my fist at the darkened heavens as I shouted my questions of "why?" Why not take me and leave them? But of course, the only reply was the silence I heard as I looked into the darkness. I ceased not only my alleluias; I stopped talking to God at all. It seemed that God was as helpless as we were in the face of the darkness. All those promises of coming light and hope died with my Rachael and Aaron. O my dear Rachael, all was not well.

The same rabbi who taught me the words of our ancient text tried to comfort me with words from the past. He told me that real faith was being able to whisper alleluia when we could not shout it. We had to trust God in the darkness as well as in the light.

I listened out of respect for him, but I knew that my silence was deep and that I had no reason any longer to have a relationship with a God who allowed so much darkness in a world that needed light. The rabbi's response to me was weak indeed when he told me that we must continue to wait patiently for the "Coming One." He assured me that the same Scriptures that seemed to fail me in my time of need promised that God would send a deliverer to shed light to his people.

I thought to myself, "Are you too going to tell me that all will be well?" I was tired of empty words.

I bowed my head and simply walked away from him and from God. I went back to my work in the small vineyard miles away from our village. I had hoped the vineyard would be my gift to Aaron for his future. Now, though my grapes still produced a small amount of wine for me to sell, their taste to me was as everything else: bitter.

And so the bitterness became almost unbearable when I heard that there would be yet another taxation. I was told that the Romans required that we must return to our home village to register. I had not been back to my home for many years. I had created a new life with Rachael and Aaron and my grapes. Though it was but a few miles to Bethlehem, I hated even the thought of returning.

I made myself go. I knew that I would have to stay the night in the local inn because I did not want to associate with any of the people from my past. I would rather be with the strangers that would be at the inn. I did not want to respond to questions or efforts to comfort me. I was beyond comforting. Darkness had become my companion and silence my language.

I arrived early knowing that the village would be crowded with others who were the victims of Roman tyranny. The innkeeper told me how lucky I was when I asked for a room for it was his last to give. "Lucky, you say?" I looked into his face and realized that he was new to that place and must have acquired the inn from the old man who used to run it when I was a child. This newcomer did not know my story, so he could assume my luck. I simply responded in a cynical whisper, "O yes, I am a lucky man all right."

I took the room at the top of a narrow set of stairs. I wanted to be alone. Later in the evening, I heard the innkeeper explaining to the countless people who came to his door that he simply had no more space. I wondered what all the people who came to register would do because the nights had become cold. They simply would have to make do. I had become used to that.

Sleep did not come easily to me ever since the night my deep darkness began so I stepped out of my room and started to go down the stairs late in the night, thinking I might take a walk. The innkeeper was again standing at the door explaining to some couple that he had no more space. I could see that the woman was very much with child. I wondered why in the world her man would have brought her with him at this time.

The thought came to me for only a moment that I should offer my room. Two years ago, I would have not hesitated. I would have made room for them, but now there was no room in my heart for a life of giving. There was only darkness and silence, so I turned away and walked back up to my room. I did not want to walk past them and have to see their faces. I wanted them to remain faceless.

I turned and wrestled with my bedroll in an effort to sleep. I somehow had the strange thought of the story of Jacob wrestling with his angel as I struggled with my blanket. But there were no angels in my barren life with whom to struggle. I tried to turn at an angle to avoid the light coming in the only window in the room. Why was there so much light on this dark night?

I stood up and looked toward the sky and noticed an exceptionally bright star. Had that always been there?

But of course it had. I almost laughed when I realized that I had long since quit looking up at the stars for light, so it could have been there any-time over these past two years and I would not have noticed. Still, it seemed strange to me that such a bright star was present in such a dim world.

I finally gave up on my effort at sleep and walked down the stairs. Rest would not come and I knew it. I might as well take one of the walks that I often took on long nights.

As I left the inn, I turned to walk toward some of the old familiar streets of Bethlehem, but I noticed a lantern hanging near the stable that was behind the inn. I looked around and the only light that was really noticeable in the darkness was that star and the light from that lantern. Interesting how you notice the light when it is so very dark.

I started to walk toward the place where my parents used to live be-fore they died. The house had been sold years before to other people. As I stepped toward the street of my childhood, I heard the soft cry of a baby. The cry came from the direction where the lantern hung. My heart froze in the silence. The last time I heard a child cry was my Aaron in his suffering. I wanted to walk away from that dreaded sound. I wanted my silence back. I needed it.

But something lured me toward the sound. Perhaps it was my heart breaking yet again at the sound of a child that beckoned me toward that light.

I looked into the stable and saw them. It was the couple who asked for a room when I turned my back on them. For the first time in years I felt something other than grief. I felt shame. What had I become? I was so lost, broken, and wounded that I could not hear the wants and needs of others? My darkness had surrounded me so much, and I was so angry at God's silence and helplessness that I myself had become silent and angry.

I stepped toward the light. The man noticed me. I started to turn away. This should be a private scene. What was I doing intruding on their sacred space? Sacred, why did I think of it as sacred? Then I remembered how sacred the birth of my Aaron was. I remembered the alleluias we sang at his day of dedication. I felt again the pain of losing something so sacred.

Then he spoke to me. I was embarrassed to even be there. Somehow, I thought perhaps he knew I was the one who had turned away at that door. But then he would not have been able to see me, but it did not matter that he did not know. What mattered all of a sudden was that I knew. And then for some reason, God showed up in my thoughts. What a time for the silent God to crawl out from behind the silence. Why did I care now that God knew of my neglect? What did God have to do with any of this except that neglect had become for me God's way of relating to this dark world?

My thoughts were interrupted by the man again saying something to me.

"What?" I asked.

He looked into my face as the light seemed to come my way. "I said, did you come because you know?"

"Know what?" I responded.

"Did you come because of the child?"

Tears came to my eyes. These were different tears than those of the past. This time it was the way he said "the child." "Did I come because of the child?" My God, man, if you only knew how lost I was because of a child.

For some unknown reason, my next response to him was beyond anything rational. It was as if the word "child" was a knife that had cut into the place where I was storing all my pain and memories. I told him my whole story. I was crying like some madman. I told him of my Aaron and my Rachael. I told him of my darkness and my anger. I told him of those haunting words of my Rachael that "all would be well."

What was I doing? This poor man did not deserve this. His wife had to deliver her baby in a stable because of my indifference, and here I was burdening him with my grief. I stopped my foolish babbling and looked through my tears to see his wife holding out something to me.

"I heard your story, my friend," she said. "Your pain is deep and your anger at God's seeming absence is understandable. I am sorry for your loss. My dear Joseph's question to you about the child must have seemed almost cruel to you."

I looked into her eyes. She must be weak from her night of labor. What a selfish and cruel person I had become. Here I stood sharing my pain with two people who were alone in their time of need because of a world full of people like me.

With the light coming over her shoulder, she walked toward me. I am not sure what really happened next. I thought I heard voices behind me. It was almost like the sound came from the sky. It was as if the stars were singing. The heavens had been silent for me for so long that I knew this must be some strange reversal of my grief teasing me or taunting me.

I was brought back to myself when she handed him to me. I looked down into her reaching arms and saw the child. His tender, silent eyes looked at me. No, how can I say this? He looked *into me*. Never, even while gazing into the face of my beloved Aaron, had I peered into such a face.

Then she spoke. "My dear lost friend, hold him in your arms. He is the one the world has been waiting for. He is the child that can fill your empty life. You may have wandered into this dark night looking for a lost child, but you have been found by a child that has come to find you. This little one is the Promised One. And God wants you to hold him just now."

I know I trembled but I knew I must be steady on my feet with what I now held in my arms. This could not be happening.

I looked down into his face. I am not sure how to say this. His face seemed, well, full of light. Was it a reflection of that bright star that I had noticed earlier, or was it simply the way the light from the lantern shone behind him?

I was lost in Bethlehem. I was lost to what love meant. But somehow in my arms I felt that love was again born into this dark world. As I held the child in my arms, I heard something move behind me. I turned to see a few sheep and a group of shepherds. Two of the shepherds looked toward me and saw the child I was holding. They said nothing but they knelt down next to the manger from which the child's mother had taken him.

"Did you come because of the child?" was the man's question. What was this music in my mind? Who was it that I held in my arms? For a moment there was something present that I had not experienced in years. As I stepped toward his mother to give her back the child, I could not believe what she whispered as she took him. She smiled at me and simply said, "Now, all will be well."

Recommended music: "All Is Well" by Michael W. Smith.

Shaped by Love

A Potter in Bethlehem

THESE HANDS SHAPE THINGS. I learned the craft from my father. His father did the same thing. Bethlehem knows our pottery. Most everyone in the village has something we shaped. I put love into what I do; it is not simply a way to make a living. When you have a piece of my pottery, you have a piece of me.

I thought of this that night I first met her. She was so young to be so lonely. Her man was beside her, but she was far from home, and a stable sure was no place to give birth. I was working late into the evening that night long ago. I went to the village well to fetch some more water to use to soften the clay. The streets were full of people who could find no other place to sleep.

Registering for taxes seems an endless demand of these Roman occupiers. Having to travel to one's place of birth to report was only another burden.

As I drew the water, I heard the cry. It was the cry of a child. It seemed to come from the stable next to the inn. I walked over to discover her for the first time. Her man was stroking her forehead that was still framed with the sweat of labor.

The child was bundled up like I often wrap my pottery when I send it to another village when someone orders a piece. I wrap it because it is fragile. This child also seemed wrapped so as not to break.

I stepped toward the light of the lantern that hung from a post and noticed that she carefully placed him in a manger as if she were preparing to send him on some journey, much like my pottery. I asked them if I could do anything for them.

She smiled at me as if she were expecting me to be there. "What do you think of my little child?" she said.

"Why, he is beautiful," I responded, "but how are you?"

"Oh, I'll manage. I'm a bit surprised it happened this way, but I suppose I should get over being surprised by God."

I wondered what she meant by this God stuff. "Do you know who he is?" she asked me. I found it to be a strange question. Why should I have any idea of who this child born in the midst of animals was?

"Ma'am, the truth is I am a potter. I spend most of time doing my work. I'm not sure why you think I might know who your child is. Maybe I've been so busy of late that you know something I don't know."

I was trying to be nice to this dear young woman. I mean, why should anyone know who her child was?

"He is the child of God," she said. "If you are a potter then you need to know that this child has come to shape the world with love."

It was then her man spoke, "Mary, I don't think this dear man understands what you are trying to say. You might want to help him out a bit."

Before she could say anything else, a group of shepherds appeared from nowhere. One of them walked right up next to me and knelt beside the manger. What in the world was this all about?

The shepherd said, "It is as the voices from the sky said it would be. The voices told us to come to a stable and find a baby lying in a manger. The voices then said that this child was the long-awaited Savior. At first, we were terribly afraid. I mean, this was unreal. But now, well, I see with my own eyes. It is real."

"Savior," I actually said the word out loud.

This Mary overheard my whisper. "Yes, Mr. Shaper of Pottery. As I told you, he has come to shape the world with love. He is the One promised in our sacred Scriptures. He is the One."

"Oh my God!" I said.

Mary laughed. "You said it well, dear potter, 'Oh my God,' for sure."

I knew about the prophecies, but along with most people in Bethlehem, I had given up on such high-sounding promises that spoke of one who would redeem his people, Israel. And now the Savior was born right here, in a stable! Could this be happening, and in my village?

I went back to my shop and completed the pieces I was working on. Two particular pieces of clay kept feeling different in my hands as I shaped them on the wheel. It was as if someone else was holding on to my hands.

Their shape was not as I first imagined. This was unusual. I always knew what shape my pottery was going to take before I ever threw the clay on the wheel. But with these two pieces, it seemed different.

A few days later, I walked back to the stable, only to find the family now in a small dwelling next to the stable. I knew the people who lived there. They must have felt compassion for Mary and her man and child. I walked up to the open door and saw a sight that I still find hard to believe.

There, standing before the couple, who were holding the baby, were these men dressed in elegant robes. One was kneeling and speaking in a tongue I did not recognize. What I did recognize was what they placed before the child. There was a small chest filled with some gold coins, and next to the chest were two urns. I recognized the smell of what seemed to be frankincense and myrrh. I knew that these were gifts usually reserved for royalty.

How did these strangers know to come to this place? As they walked past me, I sort of bowed. I did not know what else to do. I was not accustomed to these kinds of people coming to my little Bethlehem.

Then a thought came to me. I hurried back to my shop, almost running. I picked up one of the two pieces that contained within them the mystery that I had felt as I shaped them, and I placed it in a basket. Returning to the dwelling, I spoke words of greeting to the people of the house.

I walked up to Mary. "I see that word must have gotten out about your child. It seems that gifts are in order." The next thing I did was not what I had planned.

Like the stranger on his knees, I too knelt down. I was not at that time a very religious man. Oh, I went to our small synagogue occasionally, and I had made the pilgrimage to the Temple in Jerusalem a few times at Passover, but truthfully, none of it held much meaning for me until that day I knelt beside him.

I looked up into the smiling face of this Mary. "Oh, so you too bring something to my child?

I lifted up the basket and from it took one of the two cups I had shaped. "As I was making this, something was different about it all. It was as if someone was guiding me. I have never felt that way before, so here, this is for your child. Consider it shaped *by* love for one who is to shape the world *for* love." I smiled back at her.

As I gave her the cup, she handed the child to her man. Then she seemed to cradle the cup as if it were her baby. She held it close to her almost as if she was going to rock it back and forth.

Then she looked into my eyes like I have never been looked upon before. "Oh, my dear new friend, what a gift this is. As he grows up, I will tell him of a man who shaped this out of love. I will give it to him later to take with him on his journey. I am sure he will make good use of such a gift of love."

That was many years ago. I later found the grown man. I heard of him from the street talk. I listened to stories about him giving people sight and restoring health to sick people. There was even one story about him turning water to wine.

I listened to him teach every time I could find where he was speaking. And then I encountered him again that day in Jerusalem, when the men who were his closest friends asked me if I knew of a place where they could celebrate the Passover meal.

I had been selling some of my pottery at a small stand just outside the Temple gate. As they came by, I bowed, and one of them noticed this. Evidently realizing that my gesture meant that I was aware of who he was, one of the friends asked me the question about the meal.

In fact, I did have a relative in the city who I knew would be hospitable, so I arranged for them to have the Passover meal in a room above where the family lived. I even helped prepare the table that evening.

As he said the words that night over the meal, I recognized them from when my father used to say them. They were ancient words. I was standing in the doorway for I knew this meal was not for me but for them.

Then his eyes caught mine. I started to take my leave, but his eyes would not let me go. It was then that he lifted up a cup. It was my gift! The chalice I had given to Mary that night was now in his hands. He spoke strange words about a gift of love he was giving.

As he spoke, he looked first at those around the table, and then he looked over at me. Did he know? How did he know it was me who had shaped what was now in his hands? Or was this my wild imagination?

In a few days it was all over. I watched from a distance. Why did they have to kill such love? I found his mother that afternoon at the bottom of that hill of death. What had he done to deserve crucifixion? Later, I saw this same Mary again cradle her son as if he were still her little child.

I don't know what became of the cup that I made for him that he used that night. I only know I've kept the one like it that I shaped long ago, the night after he was born.

I often looked at it as I remembered the kneeling shepherds and the robed strangers with gifts. And, as I listened to Mary's child teach and offer words of hope, I thought of my cup given to him. That night when he lifted my gift to talk about love, I remembered how my hands had felt the day I shaped that cup.

What kind of gift of love was this? Mary said the night of his birth that her child was to shape the world for love. What would come of that love now?

I still remember what he said when he lifted my gift up that night at the meal with his friends. "Take . . . Drink . . . This is for you." He was giving them a gift.

And the day Mary held his broken body, I thought of my gift to her and to him. As she held him that day beside a cross, I remembered the night at the manger and how she had wrapped him like some piece of fragile pottery. I could tell from the way she cradled his broken body in her arms that he was still her little child.

Recommended music: "Still Her Little Child."
Words and music by Ray Boltz and Steve Millikan.

The Census Taker
What Counts?

IT WAS LONG AGO but I remember still. The night was cold. For a while there was even some snow. I should have known that with such a rare event the night itself would be different. That night, as I walked the streets of Bethlehem, I wondered about an exceptionally bright star whose light seemed even brighter as it reflected off the snow that clung to the trees. I knew the snow would not last so I enjoyed my walk.

Most of the people I had encountered that day would be sleeping by now. They had no use for me, and I knew their hate. My father had gotten me the job of census taker and tax collector from Quirinius. It was a favor owed my father. I was allowed to charge whatever I wanted so long as the base tax was paid by those who had to register.

Caesar Augustus was concerned about how many people were not registered. He needed more tax money for his occupying army so he had announced yet another registration. To be registered, many people had to travel long distances to return to their places of birth. To not have what I hold in my hand, registration documents, meant imprisonment. This is what counts.

I needed that job, or at least I thought I did back then. It seems so long ago now. All that is left of that old way of life is this pouch and a few of these documents that I gave to people as proof of registration.

I have to say, Esther was the cause of it all. She wanted to leave our hometown, Jericho, and its limited life. I fell in love with her and her desire to have more in life. The night she told me she was carrying my child sent fear into my heart. I knew her father was a religious zealot. What would he do?

I was surprised when he quickly agreed to have the rabbi draw up the proper papers for betrothal so that a quick marriage could happen. He wanted his first grandchild to have a last name. At that time, I was working for my father keeping records for his small business. We sold animals. It was not a bad living, but it was not what we needed for a good life.

Esther's father thought it to be enough. The marriage was arranged and months later Benjamin was born. When Esther handed him to me, I knew I needed to provide for my family better than I could in my father's business.

So, when my father told me the news that Quirinius could offer me a position in the tax office registering people and collecting taxes, I knew that we were assured of a good life. I thought Esther would be excited, but when I told her, she wept. "You cannot accept that," she said through her tears. "Our religion forbids anyone from doing such an unclean thing."

Her father screamed into my face that the money I would collect would be blood money and that if I accepted such a role, I would no longer be welcomed in his family. I thought Esther wanted an escape from this life, but I realized that she had been captured by her religion and its false promises. I was not a religious man and had no use for promises that never seemed to come true, or at least I used to be that way years ago.

I could not turn down the offer. I told Esther that I was leaving and that I would send her and our Benjamin some of the "blood money" to make sure they had what they needed. Funny how her father allowed her to take it even as he kept spouting off about a Messiah who would come and change everything.

To me it was just another empty promise. There would be no "Promised One," and the sooner the people realized that this paper I hold in my hand is what counts, the sooner they would be able to get along in life. Caesar Augustus was the only king that mattered and Quirinus was the voice they had to listen to or else. No Messiah, no Promised One would help the people.

Some of those who would not listen to this truth tried to take over the tax office in Jerusalem. Some guards were killed. Days later, the entrance-way into Jerusalem was lined with crosses. All those who participated in the rebellion were crucified and their bodies left on crosses by Caesar's soldiers to remind the people what would happen if they did not comply with the only orders that mattered from the only king that mattered. The registration that led me to Bethlehem that night so long ago was, in part, a result of Caesar's desire to make sure everyone knew to whom they owed allegiance.

I wanted so to be able to hold Benjamin, but I was no longer accepted by her family. The people hated me and what I did, but I was not a bad man, just a practical man. I sent my money, but I was not allowed to even hold or be the father to my own child.

This is what I thought about as I walked the streets of Bethlehem that cold snowy night. I thought of Benjamin and what my life would be like with a child to love. What Esther and her father did not know was that often I would help people. I would give them documents that would show what their tax should be, but I would not base their tax strictly on the number of their children but on what they could pay.

Sure, I took more from some than I did from others. I had the right to charge what I wanted, and from those I knew had enough, I took what I could. They needed what I had, and I took what I needed from them.

But it was a lonely life. As I walked that night, I could see people huddled together around fires. It was exceptionally cold and with this rare snow, people were seeking any shelter that could be found.

There was only one inn in Bethlehem. Most people had long since left this little village for there was not much of a life in it. But many had been born there, so many had to come back to register. I knew as I walked past those bundled up under trees and even in the small caves in the hills near the village that I was the reason for their discomfort that night. They knew it and so did I.

I turned to go back to the small house that was provided for me. It was the place where the people had to come to be registered, and it had one room for my needs.

As I walked past the inn, I heard a woman scream. I saw a lantern and the silhouette of man bending over and reaching for something. I thought of my Esther and what she might be doing this cold night. I wondered if the man was hurting this woman.

As I approached, I had to make my way between two donkeys and some goats who were tied to some posts. I realized that this must be the stable for the inn. What in the world were this man and woman doing in a stable, and why was she screaming?

The lantern's light seemed magnified by the snow that was still falling, so I quickly saw the reason for the woman's cries. She was in the midst of childbirth. I started to turn away, knowing that this was a private matter, relieved that the man was not doing her harm.

Then he said, "Sir, please help me. Could you hold the lantern so I can see better? I've never done this before, and my Mary needs me."

I had not even been present for Benjamin's birth. Some midwife had helped her. I should be not present for this. And if this man knew who it was he was asking help from, he would not want my help.

"Please, sir."

I held the lantern and tried to turn away so as to give this dear woman at least some of the privacy she deserved. I felt a deep sadness because I knew I was the reason this couple was having a child in a stable. They must have come to be registered, and now they needed me in the midst of their pain.

I heard the cry of a baby. I waited to turn my head until the man said, "Hand me the bowl of water, if you will." I did as he asked. Then he stood beside me and said, "Oh, thank you so much. Could you stay here with Mary while I go get some more water? I do not want to leave her alone."

I did not say anything and he did not wait. He just walked off into the night leaving footprints in the snow.

I turned toward this Mary and saw that she was now holding her child all bound with the strips of cloth that were lying across a manger when I first arrived. Her face was still wet from the time of her labor. I thought of Esther and Benjamin. He would be almost two now. I wondered if he was talking yet.

My silence was broken by her words. "Thank you so much for helping Joseph. You were an angel indeed."

"Angel," I thought to myself. "I am no angel, and if you knew who I was, you would call me something far less worthy than an angel."

I probably should have simply acknowledged her thanks and kept my mouth shut, but for some reason, I told her who I was. I did not stop there. I told her my story and shared with her my deep sadness that I was not able to be with my own child, and here I was with some strangers and their child.

Then I stopped. What in God's name was I doing? Here this woman was still hurting from childbirth. Her baby was born in a stable. I was part of her undoing. She did not deserve me sharing my agony.

Then she said, "Could you put your arm around my back and help lift me up a bit? I want to put him in this manger. Joseph found some fresh straw. It will help keep him warm."

I did as she asked. As we both looked down into the straw, she said, "Isn't he beautiful?" I did not respond. I was thinking of Benjamin.

Then she put her hand upon my cheek. "Now that I know who you are, you must know that you are still an angel to me. God can use all sorts of people, it seems. You miss your Benjamin, don't you?" Then she motioned toward the manger, "Pick him up."

I must have looked shocked because I turned away. I did not want her to see me cry. "You still remember how to hold a baby, don't you?" she said. So, I picked him up.

His warmth surprised me. It was a cold night. Why did he feel so warm? I looked into his eyes that struggled to focus on this man who held him.

"Do you know who he is?" she asked.

Well, of course, I only knew that she was Mary and her man was Joseph. Why would she ask me such a question? Then I remembered who I was. I was the one who put names down so that they would count. Maybe she was being sarcastic or something. But that did not seem to be her nature. "Well, no, I don't know who he is, of course, but I agree that he's beautiful."

Then she said, "My dearest angel, you hold in your arms the Promised One. Joseph is not his father."

Then I thought of why I felt some kinship with this couple. This Joseph was being brought into a family to give a child a last name. I knew that feeling.

"It is not what you think, my friend. This child is God's child."

Then she smiled as she took him from me and placed him back in the straw. "You see, another angel told me of his coming. I do not ask you to understand; I simply want you to believe. You are one who has to know names, right. His name is Jesus." Then she laughed a small laugh, "And you can write that down for I think others may be writing it down someday."

I thought of Esther's father who threw in my face years earlier the promise of a Coming One. I wondered what he would think now if I told him this Coming One was born on a cold night in a stable. But somehow my cynicism was overcome when I looked again at the child.

I was the one who knew what counted, but in that moment as I looked at the infant in the straw, everything turned upside down. It was long ago, but I remember still what happened in that moment. All of a sudden what counted before did not count for much. I wanted to go home. I wanted something I did not have. I wanted some peace, not a list of names.

Joseph returned with the water. As he did, I noticed a group of men walking through the still falling snow. They were shepherds. They noticed the satchel around my arm, and they started to draw back. Shepherds were notorious for not registering.

I stepped out toward them. "Don't let me stop you from coming close."

Then one of them said, "Voices in the night sky told us to come find a child who is the Promised One."

I smiled and said, "Well it seems you listened, and I think you have found him."

As they approached, I stood back, and then they knelt beside the manger. I was surprised that shepherds had any religious thoughts, but then who was I to judge them?

What I did next surprised even me. "Look, this registration is going to be something you cannot avoid. Give me your names and I'll give you some documents that will help you. It will help you avoid more taxes. Just show these and no one will say anything."

"Why are you doing this? one of them asked. "Because I can. Soon I will not be able to. I'm going home. I'm leaving this life. Somehow, I found a child tonight who helped me find me. Don't ask me to explain; just give me your names so I can give you these documents."

Then I turned to Mary. "You say his name is Jesus?" Then I took from my satchel one of my documents and I wrote their names on it. "You will need this. I'm the reason you have to have it. Take this now. I have written it so that your taxes will not increase."

"Ah, see," she said, "You are an angel after all."

"No Mary, I'm no angel, but I am going to be a father again. Somehow your Jesus helped me see something I failed to see before. I don't know why or how. You say he's the Promised One. I don't know what that means except I think I need to make some new promises about what really counts in my life."

I turned to walk away into that exceptionally bright chilly night. It had stopped snowing. I went home to my child because of that child in the straw. It was long ago, but I remember still.

Recommended music: "Straw Against the Chill."
Words by Bob Franke, sung by Kathy Mattea.

Herod

What Child Is This?

YOU MUST UNDERSTAND WHAT power is. Power is not found by gazing at stars, like those strangers the other evening seem to think it is. Power is gained, fought for, or even stolen. I understand power, and it is found at the end of a sword or perhaps in the hands of the man with the most money.

My people think that their . . . or *our* . . . religion has power and they are right, except that power must be controlled and used by one who knows what's best for them. The people are stupid and filled with false hopes. Prophets and sages have called our people sheep, and that is a good image for they are easily led.

But my sheep have learned not to mess with this shepherd. The way you keep power is to slaughter a few sheep from time to time, just to show them who is in control.

I had to beg, buy, and kill for this crown, and I'm not about to share it with some crazy, hoped-for "King of the Jews" who happens to be prophesied about in our sacred texts.

To be king of these rebellious, lost sheep, you have to have high walls and well-paid guards; you have to kill off your competition, marry well and smart, and have Rome in your pocket.

I made friends of Octavius and Anthony before they tried to kill each other off. So, when Octavius became Caesar Augustus, I hedged my bets, and Caesar repaid me by helping to defeat and execute my chief rival for this crown, Antigonus. I put his head atop a pole for all Jerusalem to see. Then I said to those who stared at the sight, "You notice that there is no crown atop Antigonus' head?" There can be only one King of the Jews, and that is Herod.

It was I that placed the high priest in office to make sure religion goes my way, and after taking my first wife to trial and having her condemned to death, I married a relative of the next high priest. Sort of a double binding you might say. There is nothing like money mixed with power and religion.

I did feel some sadness at having to put two of my sons by my first wife to the sword. But they had plotted against me! Make trouble with Herod and you die. That is what it means to be king and stay king.

Word came to me that Augustus said to one of the members of the Roman Senate that it was better to be one of Herod's dogs than one of Herod's sons. So be it. At least Augustus knows who is King of the Jews. My people call me a half-Jew because I was married into the religion rather than being born into it. They want to quote me some law of Moses about origins and birth. You are not *born* King of the Jews. You have to fight for it, no matter what those stargazers said.

Oh, don't get me wrong. I was respectful of those "seekers after truth," as they called themselves. They requested an audience with me, since these pilgrims from the east were looking for one "born King of the Jews." Perhaps they thought this new king was one of my sons. No, the only son who will wear *my* crown is Antipas. He is smart enough to stuff his rebellious spirit. He knows what I do to my offspring who do not know how to wait on power.

These men, all dressed in fine garments like they were kings of some distant land, bowed before me. They said they had been following a special alignment of stars in the night skies. They had studied ancient texts from many lands and determined through their studies that a special king was to be born in our land. At least they knew to whom to come to find a king.

One of the advisors I keep around me to help me understand this strange religion of my people helped me interpret what these strangers were asking. I looked into his priestly eyes and asked him if he knew what "Scriptures" these seekers were referring to. He looked out the window and said as if he were talking to the night sky:

"And you O Bethlehem of Judea are by no means least among the rulers of Judah, for from you shall come a ruler who will govern my people Israel."

Then he looked toward me and quickly away. He knew the danger of his words and that I might personalize them as if this was his idea. I told him, since he understood the strange language of these foreigners, to tell them that I too wondered what our ancient Scriptures meant when they foretold of one who would be a new king.

"Tell them I am the one who maintains the religion of our ancestors and that if they find this new king, it is my obligation to show him honor and respect. Tell them if they find him to come back to me that I might acknowledge his new reign."

My priestly interpreter looked awkwardly at me as I said these words, so I pointed my finger at him and said firmly, "Tell them exactly what I said."

He did as I had commanded, and the stargazers went into the night to seek this "new king."

My subjects are always wanting a new king. My spies tell me of the longing people have for a deliverer. Can't they see that I am the only deliverer they are going to get? I am the one who arbitrates between them and the Romans.

Look at what I've done for them. I've put down rebellions in their midst. Why, last year there was an uprising because I had an eagle carved into the wall of the Temple. They assumed it was the Roman eagle and went into a religious fervor. I told them it was no such thing, even though I knew it was, but I had it removed. It was a small nod their way because they are not going to get what they want. There will be no deliverer from heaven. This religion of ours is simply to help the people put up with what's going on, and I hold this power in my hand because Augustus allows it.

I am not stupid. I did not get this crown by waiting on someone else to be "king." I sent my spies ahead of these seekers from far away. Two of the spies came back last evening telling me that the only thing they could find were a few strange stories being told by some local shepherds who hang around Bethlehem. These shepherds told idle tales of the heavens igniting a few nights ago.

"What do you mean *igniting*?" I asked.

"These are shepherds, remember," my informer said. "Do you really think what they say has any merit?"

"Well, what gibberish did they utter?" I asked.

"Well, I will tell you what I heard, and you can do with it what you wish, my king.

"Supposedly, they were visited by angels who told them that a child was born in, well, in a stable. They were told they would find the child in a manger and that, well, and that this child was what they called 'Christ the Lord.'"

"Christ the Lord? . . . What is this Christ thing? Is this the same as king?"

"You'll have to ask some of your religious advisors about that. I am, after all, just a humble servant of my king."

"Yeah," I thought to myself, "you are paid for your loyalty."

I turned to the same priestly advisor who helped me interpret the words of the foreign seekers. "Is this child the same as the one the stargazers were seeking?" He did not answer. "What child is this?" I screamed.

"I have built my people a magnificent Temple. It is a wonder of the world. In it is housed their . . . or our . . . God in the gold pillared Holy of Holies. I have brought them security from the Romans. My port at Caesarea allows ships to come in bringing food and materials for theaters and other places of entertainment to help the people escape from reality for a while. Some are already calling me Herod the Great. Can't the rest of these sheep of mine listen to the truth? Why do they need to look to a child born in a feed trough to find any hope? What child is this for God's sake?!"

My advisor still did not answer. Perhaps he knew my question was not intended to be answered. My response does not depend on some foolish seekers after stars nor does it depend on shepherds telling angel stories. I am the only one who will fulfill any Scriptures around here. I am the only King of the Jews who will wear this crown. This crown does not fit a child born in a manger. What child is this?

It has been two nights since the stargazers came asking their question. My other spies have told me that whatever these seekers found, they left Bethlehem and did not come back to me. They did not know with whom they spoke. I should have them buried beneath the sands they traveled across to get to my kingdom, but I will not spend my time trying to find them. Let them follow their stars. I must take care of this new king.

There is room for only one king in this land and it is no manger child. I could not even sleep last night. I was troubled by dreams. I do not like to be troubled by dreams. Why is it that some child born in a manger even gets my attention? What child is this who is sought by stargazers?

It will all be over soon. No one will pay attention to crazy stories told by shepherds. The stargazers will return to some distant place and, I suppose, look for other signs. I know how to handle this. It will all be forgotten in a few days. This crown is not for a child. I have killed truth before. I am Herod the Great. Ha! What child is this anyway?

I know what power is. The people can have a bit of God and some of their religion, enough to keep them in their place, but I am king. Why am I even troubled by this? These false promises coming out of Bethlehem will soon be over. People will remember the Temple I built and the peace I kept. They will not remember a child born in a manger. I'll take care of that. This crown belongs to me!

Recommended music: "What Child Is This?"
Words by William C. Dix. Tune: Greensleeves.

PART 2

Advent Poetry

Please Wait

She saw only hurried faces
rushing ahead
but she told him,
"Please wait."

So when the voice said,
"No room,"
she wondered if an
angel's voice would
break the night sky.

But there was only the vacant
stare of a willing
Joseph who led
her out back.

Into all the questions
came her child
and surprised shepherds
and stars that sang
and strangers with gifts.

And as Mary looked
into the night
that reflected in
the infant's eyes
she clearly heard
the voice
of the God
who sent an angel invitation
say to all the world-
"Please wait."

Not Yet

Soon outcasts whose
only companions
are sheep
will be summoned to
a not-so-royal
court
but
not yet

Soon star gazers will
follow their hearts
and a light
only to be surprised
to find a child
cradled in
poverty
but
not yet

Soon a frightened king
will seek answers
from sacred texts
but will not find them

and will be
surrounded by
more questions
but
not yet

We, like Mary, must wait
upon the good news
for all
because waiting is
required by a
Father who
knows the impatience
of a people
who need the child
but
who also need the time
of
not yet

The waiting is a pregnant
space filled with
longing and hope
'Tis a laboring time
of listening and
preparing
Advent
the season of
not yet

An Advent Affirmation

We believe in God, who told a man named John to shout into the
wilderness,

"Prepare the Way of the Lord."

We believe in God, who sent a messenger to a young girl

and asked her to be the bearer of good news.

We believe that God needs us, like Mary, to say "yes" to the invitation
to be the ones who will continue to help God redeem the world.

We believe in the God of Joseph, who had to take a leap of faith

in order to believe the unbelievable.

We believe that the baby born in a stable is the long-awaited Savior of the
world

and that if

we follow him, everything will be different.

We believe that the Holy Spirit is an unseen power

that can enable us to do far more than we ever thought possible,

if we will but follow the lead of that Spirit.

We believe in the God of Advent, who asks us to prepare for the coming
of Jesus,

and that in that preparation,

we shall again discover the amazing love of God for us, and for our
world.

Amen.

The following are two companion poems based on the angel's visit to Mary and Joseph's response. These are offered at the beginning of the Advent journey for spiritual pilgrims who are preparing for the birth of Jesus, as Mary and Joseph had to prepare.

Beyond Impossible
(The Angel's Visit to Mary)

This whisper fills the
emptiness I feel
You say to me that
soon
I will be full
of life

But your words are
beyond impossible
My Joseph has yet
to touch me
and your words while
filling me
will leave him
empty

Can I bear this news
you share that seems
so good
yet is full of risk
and the stares

that are soon
to come?

If I say "yes" to the
hope you offer
my life will be full
of the "no's" of others
who will believe
that all of this is
beyond impossible

Yet your invitation is from
that "beyond"
where the impossible is birthed
So let it be
And I shall hope
that at least
my Joseph
will believe

It Can't Be
(Joseph's Response)

She was mine upon the asking
purchased with love
But now she has been
taken from me
by some mystical
whisper from
beyond

It can't be, for I have
longed to hold her
all the years
of my loneliness
Now my loss is full of
empty promises
broken like
the covenant I made
but days ago

I could have her banished
or worse
but then came the

angel-like dream
that left me
drained of doubt
and filled with
hope

So I will be a husband
and some kind
of adopted father
I will hold her
in the midst of
all the stares of
those who
think it is
beyond impossible

O God, who must have
done this,
you will need to give me
what I do not possess
Lift me beyond the words
"It can't be"
to those that
proclaim
"Let it be"

Still Christmas

Towers may fall and poison can fill
lives and promises of death
Still, Christmas stirs in the
ashes of buried dreams
and amidst another
desert the wind
scatters a shrill voice
"Prepare!"
Still . . . Christmas

Herods in ages past and
today try to kill the truth
Still, Christmas births itself
into waiting hearts
who long to know
that God will again
beckon voices in the stars to say,
"Behold!"
Still . . . Christmas

Too Full

So it begins in some
wilderness absent
of Christmas trees
and carols

Why such a bland start
to a journey that
leads to a
waiting manger
. . . seems strange

But the God who calls to
us from the desert
of our too full lives
knows us well

We want to unwrap
the waiting present
too soon but
we are not yet ready

There must be some
waiting and weaning

for we are addicted
to our "too much" lives

So a crusty prophet will
again call to us
to prepare a way
for "the Way"

His not so "joy to the world"
cry will challenge
our too full expectations
requiring some emptying

Mary is waiting with her
dream-struck Joseph
and Bethlehem's too full
inn waits too

For now the Advent call
is for us to wait
and watch and wonder
for we are too full
to receive God's gift

But we can make room
if we listen to
Advent's words
in the wilderness

"Prepare the way of the Lord,"
but there must be
a place and
we are too full
So again, yes again
we need Advent

PART 3

Christmas Poetry

Holding the Love of God
(Mary holding her child for the first time)

So short it seems when
a whisper from beyond
told me of
your coming

Now I hold you in my arms
for your only
cradle is one
meant for animals

Such a beginning should
not surprise me
but it does
for words cannot
hold all of this

My pain to give you birth
is a sweet joy
for I hold you now
but for a time
and now time

will hold you

for all time

O child of promise

what can I give

you more than

I already have?

I offered my innocence

in trust to a God

whose surprises

seem endless

but now I hold you

in my arms

and in my heart

Your deep dark eyes hold

starlight that seems

to peer into

my soul

But then you are from

a place beyond my imagining

I am your mother, dear one,

and as you grow

into your life

you will discover

who your father

is

For now,
feel the love I
have for you,
O child of
the manger,
At least tonight
you are mine

I will share you later
for I must . . .
For now I hold you
for me
Listen, O God,
at least for this
precious moment
your world
must wait

In Spite Of

In spite of the darkness'
claim of victory
the light came in the
midst of a night
of
chaos

"Not enough room for
the light to shine,"
screamed the darkness
but in spite of the cry
the
light was born

There in the shadows
created by a shining star
the darkness cringed
to see a child
of light
who smiled at kneeling shepherds

"How could this make
any difference?"
came the last protest
from the darkness
but
in spite of no room
and dark shadows
the light
shined in the darkness
and
the darkness
could not overcome it

So the darkness waited
for a black Friday
that would
come
all too soon

But on this night Mary
smiled as she
held her child of light
and the darkness
crawled back
into its womb
of death
for life had overtaken
the night . . .
For yes,
in spite of
it all
it was Christmas
at last

Night Sounds

There was the sound that
seemed to them
like angels singing
but imaginations run deep
with shepherds
who spend long
nights waiting
for dawn

But this night dawn came
early for the sounds
were accompanied by
dancing lights that seemed
like fire that
wanted to burn away
the fear that
filled them

"Do not be afraid," the night sounds
proclaimed
and then spoke
of great joy that would
fill all the silences

that had been
waiting to be filled
including those
of lowly shepherds

And so they made their
own night sounds with
words that said
they would go down into
the sleepy town
that was so silent
but seemed to be
waiting on them
to come

And now the child waits
for you to listen
to the night sounds
because he wants to speak
into your fear
and say to you
that angels' voices
spoke truth . . .

"Unto you is born a Savior"

Eyes Full of Light

Shepherds knelt beside
    the feeding trough
Voices still tickling their ears
    for stars had spoken
    to them telling of
        a Savior

Kings from far way
    followed a moving light
And found not what they expected
    but then after all
    the night was full
        of surprises

Herod knew full well
    who was "King"
And it was no star-child
    born in the suburbs
    with no credentials...
        'twas myth

Joseph, still full of questions
    and Mary still
fresh with pain knew
    only that everything
    had changed when
        he opened his eyes . . .
    for they were full of
        light for the darkness

Joseph Make Me a Cradle

Joseph make me a cradle—
one of wood and
the other of your
arms
Our child will need holding
but so will I
The angel's voice seems
distant now
faded by the hushed
words of neighbors
who judge me with
their eyes

But you whisper to me that
there is no time
for your craft
but that we must go
Your smile promises me
that your rough
hands will hold me
through the night

His words seem so barren

telling us of "no room"

for he knows not

who he turns

away

The cradle you could not

fashion you now

make with what is—

a manger

So cradle me Joseph with

the daring love that

listens to dreams

and obeys

The manger will hold

our child and

you can hold

me

and him

in arms that this

night seem

like God's

Tired of Waiting

To a world tired of waiting
came light from a
distant star

Unnoticed at first for
the darkness was so
vast and deep

Prophets' cries were muted
until a surprise
voice was heard in a wilderness

Laws and covenants seemed
but burdens to bear—
dry rules to observe

The waiting had created
hopelessness that
nothing would come

But God was also tired
of waiting though
the star's light took time

So one night the waiting
was over and stargazers
took a chance

Shepherds who understood
waiting thought they
heard stars singing

A young girl's waiting
ended next to
a waiting manger

Now God wonders if
you will wait
or become busy again

The star-child raises
his eyes and arms
to you to see
if you are waiting

Grow not tired of waiting-
it is there the
Word comes

Emmanuel—God with
us in
the waiting

The Wonder of It All

The wonder of it all
that God would
pick a frightened
adolescent who
dared listen to
an angel's voice

The wonder of it all
that a bewildered
carpenter would
take a chance
and believe in a dream
of impossible things

The wonder of it all
that outcasts
smelling of sheep
would be his first
and finest subjects
to kneel before him

The wonder of it all
that star seekers

would leave the certainty
of maps and risk
some vision quest to
discover a manger child

The wonder of it all
is that now we
can again hear angel
songs if we will but
listen with our hearts to
the wonder of it all

She Wrapped Him Tight

She wrapped him tight
but why?
Swaddling it was called
back then
So that legs would grow
strong and straight

But he was the child of
an angel's promise
Why go to the trouble
for he was
Surely straight from
the very start?

But no, God meant to
make him *real*
So that finally a
very stubborn
People would realize
that God was real

Emmanuel . . .
God *with us*

Wanting a White Christmas?

Again this year that old
sweet voice will echo
through our journey
toward hope

He sings of dreaming
in the midst of
his warmth of a
day filled
with snow

So it is with us as
we hear the melody
for we yearn to
know and believe that
the desert will bloom

So far away are those
stars where dreams
are often lifted
. . . so we wonder if
dreams will come true

But listen children of

all ages

A special dream was birthed

long ago though

there was no snow

God's "white Christmas" came

surrounded by sleepy

animals who wondered

about the strange

visitors who

arrived late

So when next you hear the

song, smile and

know that God's

dream is real

for you

and this world

No Room

Mary needed some room for
        answers to angel questions—
room to find a quiet place
        away from locals who
        whispered rumors
                of
        "who the father might be"

Joseph needed room for
        a steady assurance that
dreams could be trusted
        as a place to bet
        your life and faith
                that
        God could do the impossible

But there was no room
        that crowded night of fear
so God used what God
        seems to always use
        to get hope born . . .
                people
        who trust even when there
           is no room

Manger Message

Joseph, see it there
  as if it has been
       waiting
all these years
to be more than
a feeding place

Shape the hay and
  make it his
       first bed—
this manger's message
will be told
some day

For now, let him
  sleep in its
       cradling—
these quiet creatures
watch as if
they know

Hold him, manger
  as I have held
       him
these months of
waiting since my
night of angel's voice

More than these simple
animals, the hungry
world
needs what you
hold this night
of divine mystery

Hold me, Joseph, while
this manger holds
our child—
what will the world
do with this whisper
of God we offer?

Fear Not

Voices that seemed to
come from the stars
told them to
"fear not"
But the darkness
of the night
seemed so real

Herod did not listen
for he was afraid
of losing the
fleeting power
he held

An innkeeper feared the
overcrowded conditions
and the unsettled
feeling of putting
strangers in
a stable

Mary was afraid for on
this night there was
no angel voice to
still her beating heart
with words of comfort

Joseph feared that he would
not measure up
to being the kind
of father
the child would need

But still the voices spoke
the truth into
a fear-filled world
that needed
a Savior

So now for you and your fears
hear again
that announcement from
long ago
for he is here
in the midst of
all the fear

"Fear not" . . . even though

Unto us is born
a Savior

That Breath from Far Away

I'VE RECENTLY BEEN PART of some experiences that emphasized the need to stop and do deep breathing. This involves both what is called the "breath prayer" and a deep breathing exercise to help the body and the spirit relax. So I wrote this poem. I hope it is helpful as you contemplate slowing down enough to catch up to yourself. God waits for us to do this.

That breath from far away
found its home
in you
and all you were to do
was to breathe it

But you became afraid
that there would
not be enough
so your breathing became
shallow
as you started to run

Where are you going so fast
that when you arrive
. . . if you do
you will be lost

and out of breath?

Stop and listen and
you will hear
the breath
for it is within and without
and it calls you home

There is no "more"—for you
were created as enough
and the seeking is
but an illusion that somehow
you can catch your breath
by chasing after it

That which you long for
is already yours . . .
The breath that first created you
was a whisper
that you failed to hear

And if you will stop and listen
you will hear that whisper
say to you,
"You are mine
and
You are enough"

"Then the Lord God formed man from the dust of the ground, and breathed
into his nostrils the breath of life; and the man became a living being."
—Genesis 2:7

The Cradle and the Cup

Empty that first crystal
clear evening—
the wood waited
expecting
food for familiar guests

But suddenly it was
full of hope—
a manger that
became
a cradle for a child

What it held was love
for a waiting world
but the cradle was
only
the beginning of the journey

Empty was the cup
that night
he lifted it
to pour
out a covenant of healing

His lonely mind remembered
as he poured—
a story from Mary
of a cradle
filled with surprise that night

So that evening filled with words
of invitation
to "take and drink"—
he thought of
the cradle and the cup

And as he looked
into their eyes
he saw how empty
they were
and what was needed

So now again we have the
cradle and the cup
so both may be
filled anew
for a world's waiting emptiness

Emmanuel-
God with us
in
the
cradle and the cup

Deep Was the Night

Deep was the night
when shepherds discovered
what they were not
looking for

Not welcomed by townsfolk
unclean by religious
standards, they kept sheep
not rules

Accustomed to loneliness they
expected no notice
from on high for
they were too low

Yet into that deep night
there came something
like singing telling them
to fear not

But they had befriended fear—
fear of not enough
fear of steady rejection
fear of fear

So why did some proud
heavenly parent pick
such a band of
forgotten folk?

Perhaps because the manger child
was to be a shepherd
who would seek the lost
and tend the forgotten

Yes, deep was the night
only to be filled with surprise and
shepherds were the first to know

Too Late

It was too late—

  the evening was full

  and so was my inn

Foolish man he was

  who took his

  wife into a

   night too full

Her coming child pulling

  her toward pain—

  she wept so gently

So though it was too late

  I found for them

  a haven for animals

   to surround their foolish fear

It was too late

  but sleep came not

  so I ventured out

And there discovered a child

  fresh with marks of

  birth into a world for

   whom it was too late

But then she said to me,
 "Hold him O one
 who found us room."
And in my arms I looked
 into eyes that reflected
 the light of stars...and I knew
  it was not too late

Now It's Time for You to Sing

Something so big has happened
but you must seek
it in small ways

Heaven has broken open
and stardust now fills
the vacant places

Words cannot contain this
encounter of earth and sky
but words must be used

Only angelic voices can
dare speak what
might be—that now is

And so, "Gloria in Excelsis Deo"
Glory to God in the highest
fills the sky
where shepherds quake

Who are they to hear such
a shattering of all that is
for what shall be?

And yet to the lowly comes
that which will elevate all
who need to lift their heads

He is the child of the universe
born so meek that
some will pay him no mind

But listen to the song
of the stars—
They can't help but sing,
"Gloria"

For you and all he has come
so that worship can now be
of something other than
the little things we make big

Glory to God in the highest
so that the lowest will know
of love's penetrating power

'Twas not just the angels
that sang that night
but all creation felt a chorus
that shepherds found themselves
humming
so they went to a manger

Now it is time for
you to sing
for to do so is to worship a power
bigger than your small life

But for you and our world
God became a small life
that all might be lifted up

So lift your weary heads
O world that often feels
forgotten—
Christ is born

Gloria in Excelsis Deo
Glory to God in the highest
for
God became the lowest
for
you and for me

God's Ponderings

Life given as beginnings
a garden so
quickly lost

A people chosen not for
pride of nation
but to reflect
my light

Laws for their good
shared in stone
but broken all
too soon

Prophet's voices echoing
warnings of love
but ignored in
their constant wilderness

So what shall I do
to gain their
wandering attention?

I know . . .
This time I will
give them me
No more signs pointing
my way

I will make it personal
full of flesh and blood
and wrapped
in my love for them

Surrounded by surprise
this appearance
of mine
will be

An accepting woman
A bewildered man
A helpless child

Ah yes, that's what
I'll do
this time
I think I will
call it
Christmas

The Bethlehem Gazette
Rumors Abound about New Birth

RUMORS ABOUT A STRANGE happening are circulating around town this morning. In the midst of the anger and frustration about yet another Roman-required registration, some people are actually believing that the long-awaited Messiah was born in a stable last night.

While many think that such an event would be ridiculous, it just goes to show how desperate many people are for some good news in the midst of the hopeless feeling that seems to pervade the culture. One of our reporters actually happened upon the strange scene and discovered a group of shepherds kneeling beside a feeding trough for animals.

Knowing the reputation of the local shepherds, it seems quite absurd that the one who is supposed to deliver God's people from bondage would be greeted by a group that is not allowed or welcomed to come into Bethlehem. Shepherds are known for lack of cleanliness and have often been caught stealing from some of the residents who live at the edge of town.

On top of all this, part of the rumor mill includes whispers about the character of the mother of the child. Word from Nazareth tells of some of the elders in the town going to the local rabbi demanding that the woman be stoned for adultery. It was only the firm insistence of her betrothed husband that quieted the gathering storm. It seems he agreed to go ahead and take the young woman as his wife in spite of the remaining questions about exactly who the father is.

If the accusation is true about the child's lineage then surely the assertion that the child is the Messiah would be ill-founded. However, word has come to our politics editor that King Herod is troubled by this news. Why a man who holds such power as Herod would even bother with such idle tales is surprising to say the least.

Most of these rumors would probably be dismissed quickly if it were not for the discovery of a group of pilgrims from far away who inquired late last night about "where he who is born King of the Jews" might be found. These men stated that they had come from the East because of research they had conducted on the movement of a certain star. They further claimed that this particular star was a sign that a new king would be born.

Why they would travel so far based on such strange news leaves some people wondering if there just may be some truth in all this. The local innkeeper was questioned by our reporter, and his only response was, "If what they say is true, I sure feel terrible about not being able to find a place for them except in my stable."

You are reading this in the "News Around Town" section of the paper because our religion editor thinks that to print such a story is simply to add to people's false hopes. He went on to state that God surely would not do such a thing and that all of these rumors would soon be quieted by reality. I decided to include this story because, well, you never know.

Made in the USA
Columbia, SC
10 December 2019